COMPREHENSIVE RESEARCH
AND STUDY GUIDE

BLOOM'S
MAJOR
SHORT STORY
WRITERS

Eudora
Welty

EDITED AND WITH AN
INTRODUCTION BY HAROLD BLOOM

BLOOM'S MAJOR SHORT STORY WRITERS

William Faulkner

F. Scott Fitzgerald

Ernest Hemingway

O. Henry

James Joyce

Herman Melville

Flannery O'Connor

Edgar Allan Poe

J. D. Salinger

John Steinbeck

Mark Twain

Eudora Welty

BLOOM'S MAJOR WORLD POETS

Geoffrey Chaucer

Emily Dickinson

John Donne

T. S. Eliot

Robert Frost

Langston Hughes

John Milton

Edgar Allan Poe

Shakespeare's Poems & Sonnets

Alfred, Lord Tennyson

Walt Whitman

William Wordsworth

COMPREHENSIVE RESEARCH
AND STUDY GUIDE

BLOOM'S
MAJOR
SHORT STORY
WRITERS

Eudora

Welty

EDITED AND WITH AN INTRODUCTION BY HAROLD BLOOM

First Printing
1 3 5 7 9 8 6 4 2

Library of Congress Cataloging-in-Publication Data

Eudora Welty / edited and with an introduction by Harold Bloom.
cm. – (Bloom's major short story writers)
Includes bibliographical references and index.
ISBN 0-7910-5126-9 (hardcover)
1. Welty, Eudora, 1909-   — Criticism and interpretation—
Handbooks, manuals, etc.   2. Women and literature—Southern States—
History—20ᵗʰ century.   3. Welty, Eudora, 1909-   —Examinations—
Study guides.   4. Short story—Examinations—Study guides.
5. Short story—Handbooks, manuals, etc.   I. Bloom, Harold.
II. Series.
PS3545.E6Z657   1999
813'52—dc21
98-49499
CIP

Chelsea House Publishers
1974 Sproul Road, Suite 400
Broomall, PA 19008-0914

CONTRIBUTING EDITOR: Aaron Tillman

Contents

User's Guide

This volume is designed to present biographical, critical, and biblio-graphical information on the author's best-known or most important short stories. Following Harold Bloom's editor's note and introduction is a detailed biography of the author, discussing major life events and important literary accomplishments. A plot summary of each short story follows, tracing significant themes, patterns, and motifs in the work, and an annotated list of characters supplies brief information on the main characters in each story.

A selection of critical extracts, derived from previously published material from leading critics, analyzes aspects of each short story. The extracts consist of statements from the author, if available, early reviews of the work, and later evaluations up to the present. A bibliography of the author's writings (including a complete list of all books written, cowritten, edited, and translated), a list of additional books and articles on the author and the work, and an index of themes and ideas in the author's writings conclude the volume.

~

Harold Bloom is Sterling Professor of the Humanities at Yale University and Henry W. and Albert A. Berg Professor of English at the New York University Graduate School. He is the author of over 20 books and the editor of more than 30 anthologies of literary criticism.

Professor Bloom's works include *Shelley's Mythmaking* (1959), *The Visionary Company* (1961), *Blake's Apocalypse* (1963), *Yeats* (1970), *A Map of Misreading* (1975), *Kabbalah and Criticism* (1975), and *Agon: Toward a Theory of Revisionism* (1982). *The Anxiety of Influence* (1973) sets forth Professor Bloom's provocative theory of the literary relationships between the great writers and their predecessors. His most recent books include *The American Religion* (1992), *The Western Canon* (1994), *Omens of Millennium: The Gnosis of Angels, Dreams, and Resurrection* (1996), and *Shakespeare: The Invention of the Human* (1998).

Professor Bloom earned his Ph.D. from Yale University in 1955 and has served on the Yale faculty since then. He is a 1985 MacArthur Foundation Award recipient and served as the Charles Eliot Norton Professor of Poetry at Harvard University in 1987–88. He is currently the editor of other Chelsea House series in literary criticism, including BLOOM'S NOTES, BLOOM'S MAJOR POETS, MAJOR LITERARY CHARACTERS, MODERN CRITICAL VIEWS, MODERN CRITICAL INTERPRETATIONS, and WOMEN WRITERS OF ENGLISH AND THEIR WORKS.

Editor's Note

My Introduction centers upon elements of near-fantasy in "The Wide Net."

Ruth M. Vande Kieft, Welty's canonical critic, appears in this volume with five excerpts, as her views upon Welty's work are always essential.

Among the other high points are the novelist Reynolds Price on stance in Welty, and the poet-novelist Robert Penn Warren on the acuity of Welty's understanding of love. But the baker's dozen of other contributors are all replete with insight. It is one of Eudora Welty's finest powers that she educates her sympathetic critics, and enriches the multiplicity of her readers.

Introduction

HAROLD BLOOM

Eudora Welty is both a masterly storyteller and a superb prose-poet, thus combining in her art elements both populist and elitest. Like her greatest contemporaries—Faulkner, Hemingway, D.H. Lawrence—Welty educates her readers in both the freedom and the fear of a solitary inwardness. A grand humorist, Welty derives an aspect of her mode from Mark Twain's *Huckleberry Finn*, yet she is also in the tradition of Nathaniel Hawthorne, whose tales fuse Spenserian allegory with an American kind of fantasy. It seems wrong to characterize Welty as a fantasist: her art so frequently cultivates simplicity and directness. Yet she is a patient and evocative writer, who implicitly teaches the wisdom of compassion, a virtue that itself seems increasingly fantastic in pre-millennial America.

"The Wide Net," a story of delightful charm (though not to some feminist critics), returns us to Huck Finn's river-world, as a search for a supposedly drowned wife converts itself into a catfish-eating ceremony of innocence. Dragging the river results in an ecstatic series of secular epiphanies, in which the remotest possibility of death-by-water is washed away by the immediacy of the joy of being.

> When they turned off, it was still early in the pink and green fields. The fumes of morning, sweet and bitter, sprang up where they walked. The insects ticked softly, their strength in reserve; butterflies chopped the air, going to the east, and the birds flew carelessly and sang by fits and starts, not the way they did in the evening in sustained and drowsy songs.

The wide net itself, borrowed for the boisterous dragging of the Pearl River, is so wide that it catches everything. It is the wonder of Welty's art that it works, like the net, "as if there was no end in sight." This particular story could be extended without inflation or distortion: it is an open allegory, in which a realistic picnic is also a symbolic excursion. It does not matter "when you go looking for your sorrow as when you go looking for your joy"; the celebratory excursion is the same. Welty's river-revel even has a symbolic dragon in the great King of the Snakes, who stares at you but otherwise is not menacing, as there can be no evil in "The Wide Net."

Returning from the river, Welty's protagonist sees, curved over the roof of his house, "a rainbow at night," never beheld by him before. It is the emblem of this realistic fantasy, signifying that the missing wife is very much present, and waiting for him with their supper. The rainbow is small and gauzy, a pastoral revelation wholly appropriate for this genial, small masterpiece of a story. ❀

Biography of
Eudora Welty

(born 1909)

Eudora Alice Welty was born in Jackson, Mississippi, on April 13, 1909, to Mary Chestina Andrews and Christian Webb Welty. She graduated from Central High School in Jackson in the spring of 1925. After two years at Mississippi State College for Women in Columbus, Welty transferred to the University of Wisconsin, where she earned her B.A. in 1929. Welty then studied advertising at the Columbia University School of Business in New York City, but she left New York in 1931 and returned to Jackson following the death of her father.

For the next two-and-a-half years, Eudora worked for a local Jackson radio station and was the society correspondent for the Memphis-based *Commercial Appeal.* In 1933, she began working as a publicity agent for the WPA in Mississippi. During this period, she began taking unposed photographs of African Americans throughout the state, and exhibited her photos at the Lugene Gallery in New York City.

During the same year, Welty published her first short stories, "Death of a Traveling Salesman" and "Magic" in *Manuscript.* The former attracted immediate attention, and soon her short stories were receiving praise from critics such as Robert Penn Warren, Ford Madox Ford, and Katherine Anne Porter. In 1937, Welty published "A Memory" and "A Piece of News" in the *Southern Review,* and "Flowers for Marjorie" and "Lily Daw and the Three Ladies" in *Prairie Schooner.* In 1941, "A Worn Path" and "Why I Live at the P.O." appeared in the *Atlantic Monthly,* and Welty's first short-story collection, *A Curtain of Green and Other Stories,* was published. In the same year, she won the first of five O. Henry Memorial Awards for "A Worn Path." Welty published her first novel, *The Robber Bridegroom,* in 1942. That year, in addition to a second O. Henry Memorial Award for "The Wide Net," she received a Guggenheim Fellowship. She worked for six months at the *New York Times Book Review* in 1944.

A Curtain of Green and Other Stories and *The Robber Bridegroom* secured Welty's reputation for intricate, imagistic prose and moving characterizations. Her second novel, *Delta Wedding* (1946), and her short-story cycle, *The Golden Apples* (1949), received widespread acclaim; the latter is considered by some to be her masterpiece. Beginning in 1949, a renewal of her Guggenheim Fellowship took Welty to France, Italy, England, and Ireland.

Eudora Welty was elected to the National Institute of Arts and Letters in 1952. Two years later, she published a third novel, *The Ponder Heart*, for which she received the William Dean Howells Medal in 1955. The novel was adapted for Broadway in 1956. From 1958 to 1961, she served as an Honorary Consultant in Letters for the Library of Congress, and was awarded the Ingram Memorial Foundation Award in Literature in 1960.

In 1971, Welty became a member of the American Academy of Arts and Letters. She received the Gold Medal for Fiction from the National Institute of Arts and Letters and was appointed to a six-year term on the National Council of the Arts in 1972.

After more than a decade of publishing short stories and nonfiction, Welty returned to the novel with two of her most ambitious efforts, *Losing Battles* (1970) and the Pulitzer Prize–winning *The Optimist's Daughter* (1972). In addition to garnering critical acclaim, both novels made the bestseller lists, as did *The Collected Stories of Eudora Welty* (1980).

Welty has also written a book of verse, *A Flock of Guinea Hens Seen from a Car* (1970), and a substantial body of criticism and non-fiction, including the autobiographical *One Writer's Beginnings* (1984). She is among the most honored of living American writers. In addition to the Pulitzer Prize, she has received the American Book Award for *The Collected Stories*, and in 1980 she was awarded both the National Medal of Literature and the Presidential Medal of Freedom. In 1985, she received the American Association of University Women Achievement Award, and received the National Medal of Arts in 1986. In 1996, Welty was awarded France's highest civilian accolade, the French Legion of Honor award. ❀

Plot Summary of
"Death of a Traveling Salesman"

Eudora Welty's first published short story opens as R. J. Bowman, a traveling shoe salesman in Mississippi for 14 years, is driving his Ford down a rural dirt road. The afternoon is sweltering, and he is lost. He is also recovering from a severe bout of influenza, during which he was in the care of a hotel medical staff. The illness seems to have affected his heart.

Welty skillfully conveys the oppressiveness of the sun beating down upon the weakened salesman as a "long arm" that is pushing "against the top of his head, right through his hat—like the practical joke of an old drummer." The reader learns that Bowman's illness has caused feverish dreams, and he finds solace in thinking about his dead grandmother, "a comfortable soul," and about her feather bed. But before long he is again thinking about how weak and helpless he feels. He distrusts illness in the same way that unmarked roads anger him.

Bowman is not only feeling ill in the disorienting heat, but he is also extremely lonely. He has had few lasting relationships in his life, and those few seem to exist now only in his memory. Throughout this story, Welty will link Bowman's intense loneliness with his weakened physical state and erratically beating heart.

The salesman is headed to a town called Beulah, but although he has driven there before, he does not recognize any landmarks. Welty describes the remoteness of the country and Bowman's isolation as he passes fields where a few scattered workers watch him from a distance. He does not stop to ask directions because he is "not in the habit of asking the way of strangers, and these people never knew where the very roads they lived on went to."

After some time, Bowman sees from the absence of tire tracks that the road is about to end. He is heading for the edge of an embankment, and though he pulls the brake as hard as he can, it doesn't hold. Almost casually, he grabs his luggage and exits the car, stepping back on the road as the car tumbles over the embankment. Lacking the strength or the will to be angry or upset, he turns away and spots a small house on a hill. He walks toward it, stopping along the way to rest.

Upon arriving at the small house, Bowman sees a large woman standing out front polishing a lamp. Suddenly, his heart begins beating irregularly. It seems to him to be pounding loudly. Alarmed, he drops his bags and stares at the sizable woman, who seems quite old. Eventually, Bowman regains enough composure to greet her.

After stifling his urge to offer her a sales pitch on the shoes he sells, Bowman tells the woman about the mishap with his car. She tells him that Sonny, whom Bowman surmises is her son, will return shortly to help him out. Feeling increasingly weak, Bowman asks if he can wait inside the house. Once out of the scorching sun, Bowman's heartbeat returns to normal. The cool interior feels refreshing at first, but soon he begins to feel cold. He notices that there is no fire burning in the hearth and feels an intense stillness. He tries to make conversation by commenting on his selection of reasonably priced shoes, but the woman only repeats that Sonny will return soon.

Bowman learns that Sonny works for a farmer named Mr. Redmond. He is glad that he will never have to meet Redmond: "Somehow the name did not appeal to him. . . . In a flare of touchiness and anxiety, Bowman wished to avoid even mention of unknown men and their unknown farms." But then he surprises himself by continuing to speak in his regular voice, "chatty, confidential, inflected for selling shoes," asking the woman whether she and Sonny live here alone. He is equally surprised at how slowly the woman responds.

His pulse leaping again, Bowman silently watches the woman across the room, and at length Sonny enters the house with two large hounds. The woman explains Bowman's situation, while Bowman, who feels too helpless to speak for himself, simply shrugs his shoulders. Sonny gazes out the window to find Bowman's Ford before he agrees to take his mule and rescue the car.

Bowman watches through the window as Sonny leads the mule to the ravine. Alone once more with the woman, Bowman is overcome by loneliness. He imagines himself leaping up, embracing the woman, and telling her about the aching in his heart, both literal and figurative. He drifts from these thoughts to reality, "ashamed and exhausted by the thought that he might, in one more moment, have tried by simple words to communicate some strange thing— something which seemed always to have just escaped him."

The salesman begins to think about the next day, when he expects to be back on the road, and begins to feel hopeful. With a burst of enthusiasm, he responds in his standard salesman's voice when the woman tells him that Sonny has certainly hitched the car by now. But time seems to pass slowly. The sun sets and still he sits in silence, listening to his heart beating erratically. After a great while, the woman spots Sonny's figure in the distance. Sonny reenters the house and tells Bowman that he has successfully retrieved his Ford.

Bowman thanks the man, once more feeling an unmistakable pain in his heart and a flood of helplessness. Now that he is free to leave, he feels strangely like staying in the house. Sonny gruffly refuses Bowman's offer of money, saying, "We don't take money for such." Explaining that he has not fully recovered from his illness, Bowman impulsively asks whether he can stay the night. Eventually, Sonny consents and heads out to the Redmond's farm to borrow fire. Bowman begins to tremble.

When Sonny returns, they light the hearth and the lantern that the woman had been cleaning when Bowman arrived. Sonny asks his guest whether he would like a drink, to which the salesman responds heartily, "Yes sir, you bet, thanks!" But the act of having a drink is rather complicated. Sonny leads Bowman through the house and into the back yard, where the two men crawl through overgrown shrubs and dig up a jug of homemade liquor. Sonny pours some into a bottle, and they return to the house. There, they sit at the table and share the liquor while the woman prepares dinner.

Just before they begin eating, Bowman looks directly at the woman and realizes that she is not a heavy old woman after all; rather, she is young and pregnant. He realizes that she must be Sonny's wife, not his mother. He is shocked by this revelation. He understands that he is in the midst of a real family, "a marriage, a fruitful marriage. That simple thing," he thinks. "Anyone could have that."

Feeling vaguely as though he has been tricked, Bowman also feels ashamed of having imposed on the couple. Not wishing to be a bother, he says he will sleep on the floor by the hearth. He does not realize, the author remarks, that he had misunderstood the couple's intentions; they had never meant to offer him their bed in the first place. Sonny and his wife gaze at Bowman and then retire to the other room.

Bowman lies down and listens to the sounds of night: the nearby stream, the dying fire, and the sound of his own heart, which is racing again. He hears the couple breathing deeply in the next room and is filled with longing for the unborn child; he wishes it were his. He realizes that he cannot stay in the house; "he must get back to where he had been before." Still feeling weak, he puts on his coat, impulsively empties his billfold and places all the money under the lamp that is only half-cleaned, grabs his belongings, and leaves the house.

Once outside, he feels the cold air and begins to run toward the road where his car sits "in the moonlight like a boat." But he does not make it. When he reaches the road, his heart erupts in "tremendous explosions like a rifle, bang bang bang." He sinks to the road, dropping his bags, feeling as though "all of this had happened before." He tries to cover his heart with his hands to muffle the noise it makes. But no one can hear it. ❀

List of Characters in
"Death of a Traveling Salesman"

R. J. Bowman, the protagonist, is a traveling shoe salesman. Back on the road after a serious bout of influenza, he is driving through rural Mississippi headed for Beulah, but he becomes hopelessly lost. His car falls over an embankment, forcing him to seek help from two people in a small cabin on a nearby hill. He asks to spend the night there, but changes his mind and heads back out to the road, where he suffers a fatal heart attack.

The Woman lives in the cabin on the hill that R. J. Bowman approaches after he loses his car. Although Bowman first perceives her as an overweight, elderly woman, he later realizes that she is the young, pregnant wife of Sonny.

Sonny is the farmhand who retrieves Bowman's car from the ravine, supplies him with homemade liquor, and agrees to let him stay the night in his cabin. ❀

Critical Views on
"Death of a Traveling Salesman"

RUTH M. VANDE KIEFT ON THE MYSTERIES
OF EUDORA WELTY

[Ruth M. Vande Kieft is a professor of English at Queens College of the City University of New York. She is a personal friend of Eudora Welty's and has been publishing material on Welty's life and career for more than 30 years. Kieft also edited Welty's *Thirteen Stories*. In this excerpt, Kieft discusses how Welty's carefully chosen language heightens the "believability" of the scene.]

Most of all, [Welty's] style itself is the best illustration of her concern with "believability." The fusion of the elusive, insubstantial, mysterious, with what is solidly "real," can be seen in almost any passage selected at random from Miss Welty's fiction. The one chosen is a short and relatively simple description from "The Death of a Traveling Salesman." In this episode Sonny, the husband, has returned from a neighbor's with a burning stick in tongs; Bowman, the salesman, watches the wife lighting the fire and beginning preparations for supper:

> "We'll make a fire now," the woman said, taking the brand.
> When that was done she lit the lamp. It showed its dark and light. The whole room turned golden-yellow like some sort of flower, and the halls smelled of it and seemed to tremble with the quiet rush of the fire and the waving of the burning lampwick in its funnel of light.
> The woman moved among the iron pots. With the tongs she dropped hot coals on top of the iron lids. They made a set of soft vibrations, like the sound of a bell far away.
> She looked up and over at Bowman, but he could not answer. He was trembling.

In this passage the simple actions, sights and sounds, are conveyed to us sharply and precisely and yet mysteriously and evocatively, through the mind of a man who experiences an unconscious heightening of awareness, a clarity of vision, because in these closing hours of his life he is approaching his moment of revelation. He is feeling more deeply than ever before, and hence everything he sees he also feels intensely. We know that throughout the story he is in a semi-delirious state, and thus in realistic terms, we are prepared for all the adumbrations and overtones, the exaggerations, blurs, and distortions of his perception. But strange and elusive meanings are coming to him through all he sees: each act and gesture becomes almost ceremonial; each sight and sound richly allusive, portentous, beautiful, and deeply disturbing. The lamplight registers to him as both dark and light, suggesting the states of dream and reality, his feeling of the warmth, welcome and shelter of this home and his fear of being left out, as well as the chills and fever of his illness. His sense impressions are blended as the golden light seems to him like a flower with an odor that pervades the walls; the trembling, rushing, and waving of the light are also extended to include the walls, suggesting the instability and delirium of his impressions. The woman does not simply "walk" or "step": she "moves along" the iron pots, like some priestess engaged in a mysterious ritual, moving among the sacred objects; the sound of the hot coals dropped on the iron lids is muted, softly vibrating; the comparison to the sound of a bell again suggests the ceremonial resonance these simple actions have for the salesman. It is no wonder that at the end of the passage we find him trembling and speechless. Through the evocation of the language we have felt into his complex emotional state of wonder, fear, longing, sickness, pain, love: we have seen it all through his eye and experience. This is characteristically the way Miss Welty blends the inner world and outer surfaces of life—the way she sees to "believability."

—Ruth M. Vande Kieft, *Eudora Welty* (New York: Chelsea House Publishers, 1986): pp. 67–69.

Reynolds Price on the Onlooker in Eudora Welty's Fiction

[Reynolds Price is a professor at Duke University and the University of North Carolina. He is a writer of fiction, non-fiction, and poetry. His works include *Love and Work* and *The Source of Light*. In this excerpt, Price refers to the presence of the "onlooker" in Welty's fiction.]

You might say—thousands have—that the onlooker (as outsider) is the central character of modern fiction, certainly of Southern fiction for all its obsession with family, and that Miss Welty's early stories then are hardly news, her theme and vision hardly unique, hardly "necessary," just lovely over-stock. Dead-wrong, you'd be.

In the first place, her early onlookers are almost never freaks as they have so famously been in much Southern (and now Jewish) fiction and drama. (Flannery O'Connor, when questioned on the prevalence of freaks in Southern fiction, is reported to have said, "It's because Southerners know a freak when they see one.") They have mostly been "mainstream" men and women—in appearance, speech and action at least. Their visions and experiences have been far more nearly diurnal—experiences comprehensible at least to most men—than those of the characters of her two strong contemporaries, Carson McCullers and Flannery O'Connor, whose outsiders (often physical and psychic freaks) seem wrung, wrenched, from life by a famished special vision.

In the second place, the conclusions of Miss Welty's early onlookers, their deductions from looking—however individual and shaped by character, however muted in summary and statement—are unique. Their cry (with few exceptions, her salesman the most eloquent) is not the all but universal "O, lost! Make me a *member*" but something like this—"I am here alone, they are there together; I see them clearly. I do not know why and I am not happy but I *do* see, clearly. I may even understand—why I'm here, they there. Do I need or want to join them?" Such a response—and it is, in Miss Welty, always a response to vision, literal eye-sight; she has the keenest eyesight in American letters—is as strange as it is unique. Are we—onlookers to the onlookers—moved to sympathy, acceptance, consolation? Are we chilled or appalled and, if so, do we retreat into the common position?—"These people and their views are maimed, self-serving, alone because they deserve to be. Why don't they have the grace to writhe?" For our peace of mind (the satisfied reader's), there is disturbingly little writhing, only an occasional moment of solemn panic—

> "She's goin' to have a baby," said Sonny, popping a bite into his mouth.
> Bowman could not speak. He was shocked with knowing what was really in this house. A marriage, a fruitful marriage. That simple thing. Anyone could have had that.

Somehow he felt unable to be indignant or protest, although some sort of joke had certainly been played upon him. There was nothing remote or mysterious here—only something private. The only secret was the ancient communication between two people. But the memory of the woman's waiting silently by the cold hearth, of the man's stubborn journey a mile away to get fire, and how they finally brought out their food and drink and filled the room proudly with all they had to show, was suddenly too clear and too enormous within him for response. . . .

Or a thrust through the screen, like Lorenzo Dow's in "A Still Moment"—

He could understand God's giving Separateness first and then giving Love to follow and heal in its wonder; but God had reversed this, and given Love first and then Separateness, as though it did not matter to Him which came first. Perhaps it was that God never counted the moments of Time . . . did He even know of it? How to explain Time and Separateness back to God, Who had never thought of them, Who could let the whole world come to grief in a scattering moment?

But such moments are always followed by calm—Bowman's muffled death or Dow's ride onward, beneath the new moon.

—Reynolds Price, *Eudora Welty* (New York: Chelsea House Publishers, 1986): pp. 77–78.

BARBARA FIALKOWSKY ON ARTISTIC SUCCESSES AND PERSONAL FAILURES IN *A CURTAIN OF GREEN*

[Barbara Fialkowsky is a professor of English and Creative Writing at Bowling Green State University in Ohio. She has published essays on Parker Tyler and Frank O'Hara, and has published poetry in multiple literary journals, including *Shenandoah* and *New Letters*. In this excerpt, Fialkowksy explores the rootless nature of Welty's characters.]

Even Bowman, in "Death of a Traveling Salesman," has a desire or, perhaps compulsion, to see the world as an extension of his own rootlessness and his own loneliness. Perhaps, the symbols altered a bit, the stories are the same.

Traveling is Bowman's distance from humanity, his escape, finally, from himself. His sickness is as psychic as it is physical and the implication is that it is a disease of the heart. Welty gradually parts the curtain before him and Bowman discovers that the old woman is young, the boy is her husband and not her son, and their home together is fruitful and not barren:

> There was nothing remote or mysterious here—only something private. The only secret was the ancient communication between two people. But the memory of the woman's waiting silently by the cold hearth, of the man's stubborn journey a mile away to get fire, and how they finally brought out their food and drink and filled the room proudly with all they had to show, was suddenly too clear and too enormous within him for response . . .

Bowman discovered her, at the end of the road, the very thing he has spent a lifetime running from and believing could not exist: "Bowman could not speak. He was shocked with knowing what was really in this house. A marriage, a fruitful marriage."

The discovery is overwhelming. Taking his bags, Bowman runs from the house. "Just as he reached the road, where his car seemed to sit in the moonlight like a boat, his heart gave off tremendous explosions like a rifle, bang bang bang." If Mr. Marblehall wrongly thought that his living fantasy would have a far-reaching effect on humanity, so Bowman mistakenly felt his disease a pervasive one: "He covered his heart with both hands to keep anyone from hearing the noise it made. But nobody heard it."

—Barbara Fialkowski, *A Still Moment: Essays of the Art of Eudora Welty* (Metuchen, N.J.: Scarecrow Press, Inc. 1978): pp. 65–66.

PEGGY W. PRENSHAW ON A MAN'S PLACE WITHIN A WOMAN'S WORLD IN WELTY'S FICTION

[Peggy W. Prenshaw is an Honors Professor of English at the University of Southern Mississippi. She has been the editor of the *Southern Quarterly* and has published articles on many different Southern writers, from Eudora Welty to

Tennessee Williams. In this excerpt, Prenshaw discusses feminine heroism in Welty's fiction.]

Facing death, R. J. Bowman in "Death of a Traveling Salesman" craves the comfort of the hearth he discovers in a backwoods cabin. Weary and sick, he realizes how far he has wandered from home and his grandmother's feather bed. When he wrecks his car at the beginning of the story, he ironically commences his return to the maternal domain: the car comes to rest in "a tangle of immense grapevines as thick as his arm, which caught it and held it, rocked it like a grotesque child in a dark cradle." Bowman's recognition of the awful cost to the wanderer who never recovers the loving maternal world comes at the end literally with a heartburst of pain.

Only a very few of the characters in Miss Welty's fiction, female or male, steadfastly confront themselves as individuals separated from the clan, the natural life of the flesh. Some of these live out their lives in the heroic confrontation, but others move beyond the defiant, "masculine" impulse to an active acceptance of life that demonstrates a type of heroism I find expressly feminine. Of course, wise acceptance arrived at by one who has completed the task of the hero is, as Jung and Joseph Campbell have shown, typically the goal of the heroic quest. The archetypal adventure leads from the connection with the mother through the trials of initiation to an understanding of oneself and one's relation to the universe. At last, knowledge replaces ignorance, and the individual consciousness is reconciled with the universal. Clearly the consequence of such harmony is a life that contains both one's separateness in time and one's enduring link with what I have called matriarchal, imperishable world of nature.

—Peggy W. Prenshaw, *Eudora Welty* (Jackson, Miss.: University Press of Mississippi, 1979): pp. 63–64.

MICHAEL KREYLING ON MODERNISM IN WELTY'S *A CURTAIN OF GREEN AND OTHER STORIES*

[Michael Kreyling has been a Mellon Postdoctoral Fellow in English at Tulane University. He has published articles on

Welty's work in *Mississippi Quarterly* and *The Southern Review*. Here, Kreyling discusses the modern world in Welty's short story.]

"Death of a Traveling Salesman" steps forward immediately into this discussion of the modern in Welty's stories. R. J. Bowman, Harris's elder colleague, is a figure whose shadow can be found in [Joseph Wood] Krutch's *The Modern Temper:* physically and emotionally "debilitated" and "enfeebled" (Krutch's words) by the great machine of civilization that he serves, Bowman is sick unto death. On the first page of the story we know that Bowman's basic humanity has been infected by the virus of modern commercialism. He has hated his bout with influenza because illness forces him back upon his mortal humanity. He tries to declare his recovery perfect by paying the hotel doctor. And he attempts to quit his debt to his nurse similarly: "He had given the nurse a really expensive bracelet, just because she was packing up her bag and leaving." Neither gesture is meaningful, however, and Bowman goes off on his last trip with a doomed heart. He is a dying and emotionally powerless man; his feeble heart acts as emblem of both.

In Bowman's encounter with Sonny and his wife, the doom of the modern man is clearly discernible. Krutch writes that the modern wastes his life in "the successive and increasingly desperate expedients by means of which [he], the ambitious animal, endeavors to postpone the inevitable realization that living is merely a physiological process with only a physiological meaning and that it is most satisfactorily conducted by creatures who never feel the need to attempt to give it any other." When Bowman meets Sonny and his wife, their creatures (mules and dogs), and their contentment within a closed circle of food, warmth, procreation, and work, he is stricken with the simplicity of the other life: "A marriage, a fruitful marriage. That simple thing. Anyone could have had that." Yet there is nothing more remote from the reach of Bowman's flickering life, and never was. In feeble gratitude for their sharing, he can think only of footwear and money. In his solitary death, the modern is warned of his eventual death as well.

—Michael Kreyling, *Critical Essays on Eudora Welty* (Boston: G. K. Hall & Co., 1989): pp. 22–23.

ALBERT J. DEVLIN ON EUDORA WELTY'S MISSISSIPPI

[Albert J. Devlin is a professor English at the University of Missouri. He has published numerous articles and delivered multiple lectures on Eudora Welty. His book, *Eudora Welty's Chronicle: A Story of Mississippi Life,* was published in 1983. In this extract, Devlin remarks on the agrarian elements in "Death of a Traveling Salesman."]

In constructing a "counter-myth" to the national credo of progress, the writers of *I'll Take My Stand* agreed that Agrarianism rests upon a series of interlocking dichotomies which culminates in the formula "Agrarian *versus* Industrial." Apparently, Welty adopts a similar tension in organizing "Death of a Traveling Salesman." R. J. Bowman hopes to reach his destination "by dark," but as the "graveled road" gives way to a "rutted dirt path," the painful admission grows that "he was simply lost." A bright winter sun pushes "against the top of his head," intensifying the strange perspective from which Bowman views his unfamiliar world "after a long siege of influenza." When his dusty Ford falls into "a tangle of immense grapevines," he can only make the admission complete and seek help at a nearby cabin. Here he finds the same kind of traditional family life, marked by unvarying domestic patterns and lived in conformity with nature, that the Agrarians proposed as an antidote to mass culture. But soon after entering this rustic cabin, R. J. Bowman senses a "quiet, cool danger," for the fruitful ways of husband and wife now underline the futility of his own life of relentless travel and brief commercial encounters. In Agrarian terms, this apostle of "personal salesmanship" epitomizes "modern man [who] has lost his sense of vocation" when Bowman traces Sonny's "old military coat" to a more distant campaign than World War I. Welty's imagination may seem to be completely captivated by the Agrarian reading of history. In *Jefferson Davis: His Rise and Fall* (1929), Allen Tate boldly, if not wishfully, declared that "all European history since the Reformation was concentrated in the war between the North and the South." With less pomp, the authors of *I'll Take My Stand* endorsed this same judgment, finding in "the irrepressible conflict" between egalitarian and conservative societies a routing of traditional southern values. By asserting its progressive temper, America had deflected the Old South from its agrarian ideal. The "precious thing" that was lost apparently moved

Eudora Welty to picture "an alien commercial drive" still assaulting the last reserves of provincialism.

—Albert J. Devlin, *Eudora Welty's Chronicle: A Story of Mississippi Life* (Jackson, Miss: University Press of Mississippi, 1983): pp. 12–13.

Plot Summary of
"Why I Live at the P.O."

Welty's short story begins as the narrator, who is referred to as "Sister" by the other characters, informs the reader about her family situation. She has been living with her mother, grandfather, and uncle in apparent peace until her "spoiled" younger sister, Stella-Rondo, separated from her husband and returned to the family home in China Grove, Mississippi. The story is driven by Sister's hilariously vindictive narrative of the events that occurred over the Fourth of July holiday that led her to leave home and live in the back of the town post office where she works.

Sister says that Stella-Rondo surprised the entire family when she came back home "from one of those towns up in Illinois" with a two-year-old daughter named Shirley-T. Stella-Rondo claims that the child is adopted, a fact that is repeatedly questioned by the narrator. She claims that the baby would look exactly like Papa-Daddy, her own grandfather, if he were to cut off his beard. Stella-Rondo becomes upset by the insinuation that she is a liar, and warns her sister never to mention anything about her child again. The narrator agrees, but remarks that the child looks like a cross between Papa-Daddy and Stella-Rondo's husband, Mr. Whitaker, who was once Sister's boyfriend.

At dinner that night, Sister says, Stella-Rondo tells Papa-Daddy that Sister "fails to understand why you don't cut off your beard," and she blames Stella-Rondo for turning Papa-Daddy against her with that comment. While she provides a detailed and highly subjective account of Papa-Daddy's reaction, she also provides side remarks about him: "He's real rich. Mama says he is, he says he isn't." Welty's use of this multilevel narrative technique emphasizes both the comic and human aspects of Sister's eccentric family.

The reader learns through Papa-Daddy's reaction that he was responsible for getting her the position of postmistress at China Grove's post office. Sister confirms that she has always been grateful for her job at the P.O., despite the fact that it is the "next to smallest P.O. in the state of Mississippi." After leaving the dinner table, Sister sees her Uncle Rondo walking down the hall dressed in Stella-

Rondo's "flesh-colored" kimono, claiming that he has been poisoned. She informs the reader that Uncle Rondo drinks a bottle of "prescription" medicine every Fourth of July holiday, and he is now on his way outside to pass out on the hammock. But Papa-Daddy has gotten there first. Sister predicts that Uncle Rondo will fall on Papa-Daddy, and Papa-Daddy will immediately try to turn Uncle Rondo against her.

Meanwhile, Stella-Rondo calls from an upstairs window to Sister. She asks why Uncle Rondo is wearing her kimono, which was part of her bridal trousseau, and declares that he looks like a fool. Mr. Whitaker, Stella-Rondo says, has taken dozens of pictures of her wearing that exact article of clothing. According to Sister's account, she replies to Stella-Rondo's criticism of Uncle Rondo by saying that he is doing the best he can. She pauses in her story to remind the listener that she is defending her uncle.

Sister then heads to the kitchen to prepare some green-tomato pickle ("Somebody had to do it," she declared). There she meets up with Mama, and she argues that had she been the one to return home with a two-year-old child, she would not have been as well-received as Stella-Rondo was. She and Mama disagree over whether Stella-Rondo's child is truly adopted. Sister claims that Stella-Rondo is simply too "stuck-up" to admit that Shirley-T is her biological daughter. The argument escalates when Sister mentions a deceased member of the family whom her mother warned her against ever bringing up again. Mama slaps Sister, who launches into another narrative aside. "You ought to see Mama," she says, "she weighs two hundred pounds and has really tiny feet."

Now Sister suggests that Shirley-T is somehow mentally deficient, since none of them have heard her speak. Mama is shocked at this implication and, forgetting her vow to take Stella-Rondo at her word, recalls that Mr. Whitaker drank a great deal of alcohol, and what she believed were "*chemicals.*" Mama then marches upstairs to confront Stella-Rondo about the supposedly mute child. After Stella-Rondo expresses her extreme displeasure with Sister, Shirley-T bursts into song in what the narrator calls "the loudest Yankee voice I ever heard in my life." Mama demands that Sister apologize to Stella-Rondo and Shirley-T, but Sister refuses. She remarks that now Stella-Rondo has managed to turn everyone in the house against her except Uncle Rondo.

Sister then tells the reader how she tried at the dinner table that night to "be considerate" and get Uncle Rondo to remove Stella-Rondo's kimono before he stained it. But Stella-Rondo declares that Sister has been making fun of him all afternoon. Sister denies the allegations and recommends that Uncle Rondo lie down, but he takes offense. He takes revenge on her early the next morning, says the narrator, by throwing an entire package of firecrackers into her room while she is sleeping, knowing full well that she is "terribly susceptible to noise of any kind." After that, Sister declares, it took but a minute to decide to move out of the house.

Being as obvious as she can, she marches through the house collecting various articles that she claims are hers. She takes the electric fan, snatches a needlepoint pillow out from behind Papa-Daddy where he sits, takes a charm bracelet out of Stella-Rondo's dresser drawer, and begins digging up some plants in the front yard. When Mama stops her, she declares that she's at least taking the fern, because Mama "can't stand there and deny" that Sister was the one who watered it. She grabs a radio, some watermelon-rind preserves, and a sewing machine motor that she "helped pay the most on." She tells her family that if they want to see any of these things again, they will have to come to the post office, for that is where she plans to live. They all vow never to enter the P.O. again.

In a heated argument, Sister reveals that she reads the postcards that Mr. Whitaker sends to Stella-Rondo, so she knows everything that is going on. She points out that if they refuse to use the post office, they will have no contact with Mr. Whitaker, and he will never know when to return for Stella-Rondo. Stella-Rondo starts to cry, and Sister grabs the kitchen clock and heads for the post office, employing a child with a wagon to help her carry her belongings.

The story concludes as the narrator explains that she and her family have not seen one another for five days and nights. She suspects that they have been saying horrible things about her, but claims not to care, since she has her own mind and can draw her own conclusions. The town residents may take sides over this family dispute, Sister says, but she knows "which is which" among those who come by the post office. She closes by stating how happy she is, and declaring that even if Stella-Rondo tried to explain what happened between her and Mr. Whitaker, Sister would cover her ears and "refuse to listen." ❀

List of Characters in
"Why I Live at the P.O."

Sister is the vindictive and jealous narrator, who relates the circumstances that lead her to move out of the family house and into the back of the local post office. She blames this turn of events on her younger sister, Stella-Rondo, who recently returned home after separating from her husband.

Stella-Rondo is the narrator's younger sister, who returns home after separating from her husband. She surprises the family by bringing a two-year-old child, Shirley-T, with her, whom she claims to have adopted. The unknown heritage of this child is at the core of numerous family squabbles that result in Sister's moving.

Mama is the mother of Sister (the narrator) and Stella-Rondo. She refuses to acknowledge that Shirley-T may be her daughter's biological child, and appears to side with Stella-Rondo against Sister.

Papa-Daddy, the family patriarch, is the father of Mama and grandfather of Stella-Rondo and Sister. He has apparently helped Sister get her job as postmistress of China Grove.

Uncle Rondo, Mama's brother, wears his niece's robe and indulges in great quantities of "prescription medication." He apparently throws firecrackers in Sister's bedroom while she sleeps. According to the narrator, he is the last family member to turn against her, prompting her move out of the house. ❀

Critical Views on
"Why I Live at the P.O."

RUTH M. VANDE KIEFT ON THE RIGID CHARACTERS
IN "WHY I LIVE AT THE P.O.

[Ruth M. Vande Kieft is a professor of English at Queens College of the City University of New York. She is a personal friend of Eudora Welty's and has been publishing material on Welty's life and career for more than 30 years. Kieft also edited Welty's *Thirteen Stories*. In this excerpt, Vande Kieft discusses the rigidity of the characters in Welty's short story and how this quality creates humor.]

[A] modern type of comedy which appears in Miss Welty's fiction concentrates upon eccentric characters who follow out their natures in humorous, repetitive action. Her best known story in this mode is "Why I Live at the P.O." The analytical terms of Henri Bergson, in his famous essay on "Laughter," are applicable to this story. According to Bergson, anything is laughable in a human being which suggests rigidity—the apparent mechanization of the human body or mind—so that his gestures, actions, ideas seem to become puppet-like, automatic and repetitive, rather than living, mobile, flexible.

The rigidity of the postmistress of China Grove takes the form of an *ideé fixe*. She follows up her single idea with relentless logic until it puts her in rebellious isolation from the world about her (the "world" being, in that small town, mostly her own family). Though acting and thinking with the insane logic of the paranoid, she is not felt to be so because of the marvelous energy, self-possession, and resourcefulness with which she carries out her revenge (so that our pity is not aroused), and because of the inescapable comedy in her situation, the members of her family and their behavior, and her mode of telling her story.

The motive of her particular obsession is as clear as it is unadmitted: vindictive jealousy of her sister. Stella-Rondo has repeatedly aggrieved and insulted her: by being a younger, favored sister; by stealing and running off with her boyfriend, Mr. Whitaker, the northern photographer; by reappearing not long afterwards with a two-year old "adopted" child; and finally, as she supposes, by setting the rest of the family against her, one by one. Her story is built on the logic of that steady progress of alienations: what Stella-Rondo did to bring them about, how she herself reacted to the mounting persecution—now with admirable forbearance, now with pacifying explanations, now with righteous indignation—and all the time with the assumed burden of running the family on that hot, hectic Fourth of July.

When the process of Stella-Rondo's evil machinations is complete and everyone is set against her, she saves her pride by moving out to the "P. O." Again she works with inexorable logic, disrupting the family as she systematically removes from the house everything that belongs to her: electric fan, needlepoint pillow, radio, sewing-machine motor, calendar, thermometer, canned goods, wall vases, and even a fern growing outside the house which she feels is right-fully hers because she watered it. Finally she is left alone at the "P.O.," secure in her knowledge of who in the town is for her and who against her; protesting loudly her independence and happiness, she works her revenge by shutting her family off from the outside world.

Her monologue is comic not only because of the apparent illogic of her logic, but because of her manner of speaking. One can see the fierce indignant gleam in her eye as the stream of natural southern idiom flows out of her; it is at once elliptical and baroque, full of irrelevancies, redolent of a way of life, a set of expressions, of preju-dices, interests, problems, and human reactions which swiftly convey to the reader a comic and satiric portrait of this Mississippi family. The effect of "Why I Live at the P. O." depends not simply on the vividness of evoked scenes and sounds, but also on the implications of vulgarity which counter the comedy of the monologue in an ironic way. Marriage and family life are given their direction by the cheapest advertising, movies, and radio. Allusions to the "gorgeous Add-a-Pearl necklace," to the flesh-colored kimono "all cut on the bias" which was part of Stella-Rondo's trousseau, to the "Kress tweezers" she uses to pluck her eyebrows and to Shirley-T, her tap-dancing, and her head-splitting rendition of "OE'm Pop-OE the Sailor-r-r Ma-a-an!" suggest some of the more macabre satiric effects of "Petrified Man."

—Ruth M. Vande Kieft, *Eudora Welty* (Boston: Twayne Publishers, 1962): pp. 67–69.

Nell Ann Pickett on Colloquialism and Style in "Why I Live at the P.O."

[Nell Ann Pickett has published articles on Eudora Welty in various literary journals, including *Mississippi Quarterly*. Here, Pickett focuses on Welty's use of colloquialism as irony in "Why I Live at the P.O."]

In "Why I Live at the P. O." Miss Welty has artfully blended the techniques of humor with her colloquial style of writing. An examination of that style will show how she achieves the humorous effects through irony, word manipulation, oblique details, fallacies in logic, and characterization.

The piece is a monologue with Sister, the narrator, concerned only with external actions that justify her decision to move out of the family home. As she rails away at her family, especially at her recently returned sister, Stella-Rondo, she reveals her insatiable jealousy because a traveling photographer, Joe Whitaker, "the only man ever dropped down in China Grove," chose the younger sister for marriage. Sister acts like a spiteful adolescent and verges on the vicious in her snide remarks about Shirley-T, "that very peculiar child that Stella-Rondo says is adopted," and about Mr. Whitaker, the now estranged husband. Sister's step-by-step explanation of each incident leading up to her move to the post office convinces us not that her family has mistreated her but rather that Sister is deceiving herself. Her self-deception and her unwitting self-revelation provide the central irony of the story.

There are a number of ironic situations. In view of the outcome of Stella-Rondo's marriage to Mr. Whitaker, Sister's jealousy of Stella-Rondo is ironic. Mr. Whitaker, the stock "transient professional," who woos the available females and gets one of them pregnant, subsequently deserts his wife (there is no evidence, however, of a marriage license) and child. It is ironic and therefore humorous to us that Sister does not realize that but for the grace of allegedly being one-sided she might be in Stella-Rondo's undesirable position: having nowhere to go except home after having been left by her husband and having to explain her child Shirley-T as adopted to avoid the embarrassment of admitting the all too brief marriage-birth time gap.

Other ironic situations arise upon Sister's actually moving into the post office. As she says:

> But oh, I like it here. It's ideal as I've been saying. You see, I've got everything cater cornered, the way I like it. Hear the radio? All the war news. Radio, sewing machine, book ends, ironing board and that great big piano lamp—peace, that's what I like. Butterbean vines planted all along the front where the strings are.
>
> Of course, there's not much mail. My family are naturally the main people in China Grove.

In spite of Sister's protestations that she is happy, she reveals in her continuing childish jealousy of Stella-Rondo that she is miserable, that she has not changed:

> And if Stella-Rondo should come to me this minute, on bended knees, and attempt to explain the incidents of her life with Mr. Whitaker, I'd simply put my fingers in both my ears and refuse to listen.

Ironically, moving to the P. O. has not solved Sister's problems. And ironically, too, there is the possibility of the post office becoming defunct. Since Sister's family are, or rather were, the principal customers, the existence of "the next to smallest P. O. in the entire state of Mississippi" may be shortlived.

> —Nell Ann Pickett, "Colloquialism as a Style in the First-Person-Narrator Fiction of Eudora Welty," *Mississippi Quarterly* 26, no. 4 (Fall 1973): pp. 572–73.

ELMO HOWARD ON EUDORA WELTY AND THE CITY OF MAN

[Elmo Howell has published essays in various literary journals and was a contributor to an anthologized collection of essays on Eudora Welty. In this extract, Howell discusses the individual's relationship to society in Welty's short stories.]

When Jane Austen died in 1817, Walter Scott wrote a tribute in which he summed up the difference between her fiction and his own. He could do . . . the marshalling of events and sweep of history, but not the intimate play of daily domestic life, which Miss Austen did so well. Eudora Welty admires Jane Austen and owes much to her, indeed stands in the same relation to fellow-Mississippian William Faulkner that Austen stood to Scott. With little interest in history or social themes, she concentrates on the ordinary people of her country who go about the business of loving and hating and talking about their neighbors as if there were nothing more important in the world. But within this close range, she scrutinizes her subject and registers its vibrations with a tenderness of attention that places her closer to the heartbeat of her region than Faulkner himself.

If she shows greater variation than her eighteenth-century predecessor, it is not because her aim is different but because she lives in another age and her work inevitably shows it. Like Miss Austen, she remains aloof from social and political events of her time, but with one important difference. In spite of the French Revolution and Napoleon, England was confident and self-contained, and the Catherines, Elizabeths, and Emmas could go on flirting and finding husbands in a way of life that was apparently immutable. After two hundred years, even though Miss Welty's village remains intact, the world outside is not, and disturbing voices are beginning to be heard. Instead of writing about home and social ties, the old standbys of the English novel, young writers today are peering, in Miss Welty's words, through "knot-holes of isolation."

She does not take much to isolation—as no one could who believes in the family as she does—but feels very keenly the plight of the individual who pursues his own dream, never quite going the whole way perhaps but suffering from loneliness even while playing his part in the family life. Thus in the midst of what appears light comedy, she shifts abruptly to the subjective, and at times in fact appears uncertain where her main interest lies, with the individual or the social circle he belongs to. She veers from characters like Miss Eckhardt and Miss Julia Mortimer and the other seekers of "the golden apples" to the village at large, loud with clatter of ordinary life. Jane Austen's interest could not have been so divided because her audience would not have tolerated the private eye in fiction. She keeps passion offstage, concealed in a social mode, and so achieves a syntheses that Miss Welty's fiction lacks.

The gulf between "June Recital" and "Why I Live at the P. O.," for example, is very great indeed. One is in the major, the other a minor key. Miss Eckhardt, Virgie Rainey, and Cassie Morrison are tragic figures, while in the other story Miss Welty is out for fun and the reader is not asked to consider what lies behind the old maid's spiteful antics. These disparities, however, are more apparent than real. In the long view, as one takes leave of a Welty story, the private voice is lost in the hubbub of family or community at large: the vision is essentially social. Whatever problems the individual may have—and they are sometimes very great indeed—can best be dealt with among those he knows best in some sort of conformity to the general pattern.

—Elmo Howell, *Critical Essays on Eudora Welty* (Boston: G. K. Hall & Co. 1989): pp. 268–69.

RUTH M. VANDE KIEFT ON THE VALUE OF COMEDY IN WELTY'S FICTION

[Ruth M. Vande Kieft is a professor of English at Queens College of the City University of New York. She is a personal friend of Eudora Welty's and has been publishing material on Welty's life and career for more than 30 years. Kieft also edited Welty's *Thirteen Stories*. In this excerpt, Vande Kieft examines the weight of comic elements in Welty's fiction.]

An over-valuing of the comedy, though innocent enough, may lead to blind spots when it comes to Welty's work. Or it may have results the other way around. This is where the other delphic maxim comes in: know thyself. Readers may fall into all sorts of personal and group fallacies because they are from the South or North, of such and such a class, religious believers or agnostics, men or women, black or white, married or single, survivors of psychoanalysis or self-therapists, and so on. Accidents of nature and experience affect our explorations of meaning. Perhaps the best way to deal with them is forthrightly, as Peggy Prenshaw did in her introduction to her article, "Woman's World, Man's Place":

I feel somewhat uncertain of the boundary of my perceiving and the stories' showing. Teaching that I am, ordinarily I duck the old ontological problem and proclaim myself the ideal reader Cleanth Brooks has tried to teach us how to be. Now, however, an admission of wariness seems in order, for I am anxious about the topography I have mapped here, about the announcement that Miss Welty's fiction reveals a woman's world. It sounds distinctly like the report of a new feminist critic, but perhaps that is what I am.

Such candor is refreshing and rare.

Meaning may be a problem because it is often difficult to catch precisely the tone of Eudora Welty's fiction, to determine what Wayne Booth would call the "reliability" of her narrators. Then there are rapid shifts between and among some of the traditional generic modes of comedy, tragedy, satire, farce, melodrama, fantasy, and so on. We know about the terror adjoining the comedy in her fiction, and it rarely seems possible to think of her stories as wearing, unequivocally, one or the other of the two masks of ancient Greek drama. But it is useful to do this, occasionally, by way of testing our critical truth. First, the comic mask.

It is always interesting to see what a critic makes of Eudora Welty's comedy—and encouraging, in a way, to remember that what might be called the Ur-blooper of Welty criticism was committed by the highly discriminating writer who first introduced Eudora Welty to the world in her introduction to *A Curtain of Green*. Katherine Anne Porter called the heroine of "Why I Live at the P.O." "a terrifying case of dementia praecox." Even translating the diagnosis into what it would now be—paranoid schizophrenia—we are no closer to the truth of *that* story. This mistress of China Grove's P.O. is a case all right, but not a terrifying case history. The story *is* essentially comic; to approach it clinically or as anything but lightly amoral would, I think, be a mistake.

—Ruth M. Vande Kieft, *Critical Essays on Eudora Welty* (Boston: G. K. Hall & Co., 1989): pp. 299–300.

PETER SCHMIDT ON EUDORA WELTY
AND WOMEN'S COMEDY

[Peter Schmidt is a professor at Swarthmore College in
Pennsylvania. He received a research grant from Swarthmore to write a book on Eudora Welty's short fiction. In
this excerpt, Schmidt discusses the contrasting elements of
Welty's comic fiction.]

One way to think of the Rondo family in "Why I Live at the P.O." is
as an exceptionally noisy family of paper cutouts. Certainly the characters are as delightfully two-dimensional, and as farcically posed, as
the cutouts described in "*Women!!*" but the story is also a comedy
about fashion, gender differences, and power.

"Why I Live at the P. O." is set in China Grove, Mississippi, and
features Sister as the narrator, Stella-Rondo (her younger sister),
Papa-Daddy (Sister's grandfather), Mama (Sister's mother), Uncle
Rondo, Stella-Rondo's two-year-old daughter Shirley-T, and (briefly)
a dying woman named Old Jep Patterson. In the beginning of
Sister's monologue, most readers tend to share Sister's view of the
absurdity of her family members. Sister's main tactic is to show how
false their language is. Stella-Rondo, Shirley-T, Mama, Papa-Daddy,
and Uncle Rondo all speak an inflated language filled with
euphemisms and the brand names of fashionable commercial prod-
ucts. When Stella-Rondo displays the clothes she has brought home
for example, she shows her sister something she has never seen
before—a kimono that "happens to be part of my trousseau, and
Mr. Whitaker took several dozen photographs of me in it." By
replacing her sister's ignorance with exotic and fashionable words
such as "kimono" and "trousseau," Stella-Rondo reminds Sister that
although she may be older and have a job at the P.O., it is her
younger sister Stella-Rondo who married the man they both dated
and who escaped to live in the wide world. Thus she plays the
sophisticated, well-traveled belle, full of polite condescension and a
histrionic sense of martyrdom. In relating her versions of these
events, however, it is Sister and not Stella-Rondo who has the last
word: the kimono becomes "a terrible-looking flesh-colored con-
traption I wouldn't be found dead in." Sister uses a similar tactic
when relaying Papa-Daddy's speech to us. "This is the bear I started
growing on the Coast when I was fifteen years old," Papa-Daddy

boasts, but Sister deflates this boast with the comment, "he would have gone till nightfall if Shirley-T hadn't lost the Milky Way she ate in Cairo." All these examples are insults made after the fact, private acts of revenge taken during the retelling of the events to make up for her not being able to have her say earlier. Many of the most delightfully vulgar commercial references in the story, such as Shirley-T's Milky Way and the Add-a-Pearl necklace, furthermore, were not in Welty's early draft of the story; neither was fancy vocabulary like "disport" and "trousseau" (originally, merely "eat" and "underwear"). In revising, Welty carefully highlighted the story's comic contrasts of diction.

—Peter Schmidt, *The Heart of the Story: Eudora Welty's Short Fiction* (Jackson, Miss.: University Press of Mississippi, 1989): pp. 112–13.

Plot Summary of
"The Wide Net"

The title story of Welty's second collection of short stories describes the events that occur after a young husband assembles a group of townspeople to drag the river for the body of his wife, a supposed suicide victim. Although they do not find a body, both the husband and the rescue party end up enjoying the pleasures of a beautiful fall day.

"The Wide Net" opens early on an October morning as William Wallace Jamieson returns home after a night out with his friends. When he walks into his house, he realizes that his pregnant wife, Hazel, is not home. He finds only a note in her handwriting on the kitchen table, which says that she has gone to the river to drown herself because he has treated her poorly by staying out all night. Despite Hazel's morbid fear of the water, William Wallace firmly believes that she is capable of such an act. He runs after Virgil Thomas, one of the friends with whom he spent the night, and asks him to help look for her.

Assuming the worst has already occurred, William determines that they need a wide net and some townspeople to help them drag the river for his wife's body. During William's conversation with Virgil, the reader learns that William has been married to Hazel for a year. He reminisces about their first meeting, talks about her beauty and intelligence, and worries that Hazel's mother, whom he believes has had it in for him, will "come after" him when she hears about the drowning. He berates himself for his behavior, and speculates that Hazel chose drowning to "make it worse" but can't see how she brought herself to do it. Virgil suggests that she jumped in backwards.

At this point Welty introduces the first of many diversions that will distract the characters in "The Wide Net" from their original intent. William spies a rabbit and, filled with "a descent of energy," catches it barehanded, then lets it go. "Was you out catching cotton-tails, or was you out catching your wife?" Virgil scolds. "I come along to keep you on the track."

William and Virgil decide to recruit some members of the Malone and Doyle families and a couple black children. Instead, the entire Malone and Doyle families show up, as well as two white children who lost their father by drowning and two black children who happen to come upon the group. The crowd makes its way to the home of Old Doc, who owns the net they will use for the search.

William Wallace explains the situation to Doc, who seems to suggest that she may have run away. William asks whether he thinks she was carried off by gypsies. Comically, Doc dispels this notion by raising the fact that the gypsies would be hoping for a ransom from William, who doesn't have much to offer. When the crowd quiets down, Doc says that although he thinks they should "let well enough alone," he will go with them to drag the river.

Welty describes the group making its way to the river through a trail in the woods as "a little festival procession," of which every step "started up a little life, a little flight." Doc describes the changing of the seasons from summer to fall, and describes this day as golden. Hearing this, William thinks about his wife, "like a piece of pure gold, too precious to touch." When they reach the river, William oddly asks its name, even though he knows it and has fished in it all his life.

Part two begins as the group stretches the net between the river-banks and begins to drag the Pearl River. Along the way, they catch countless fish and eel. They come across a family of alligators that they let pass, then catch a baby alligator—an exciting moment for the group, since the Malones claim that they will bring the animal home. They find a woman's necklace and give it to Sam and Robbie Bell, the black children. They encounter a stranger fishing on the bank and turn him away. They become almost festive as they continue to drag the net.

Occasionally, William dives to the river bottom to search for Hazel. The darkest point of the story occurs when, during one dive, he goes so deep that "it was no longer the muddy world of the upper river but the dark clear world of deepness. . . . Had he suspected down there, like some secret, the real, the true trouble that Hazel had fallen into, about which words in a letter could not speak[?]"

At midday, the group pauses to eat a lunch of grilled catfish, which they prepare along the riverbank. William and the others fall asleep, but then William leaps up and begins a frenzied dance, a catfish hooked to his belt and tears of laughter streaming down his face. The group's attention is suddenly drawn to the river, where a huge snake has been spotted. Suddenly, it begins to storm.

The searchers take refuge on a sandbar during the thunderstorm and watch a huge nearby tree split and burst into flames after lightning strikes it. They become covered with wet leaves. Virgil points out that they have reached the nearby town of Dover. William cuts his foot on a sharp rock.

Part three opens as the members of the search party walk through Dover carrying strings of fish, the baby alligator, and the net. Again, the scene is reminiscent of a festival. William Wallace, who holds up a "great string of fish," ultimately gives them away to townspeople who wish to buy them. "I don't want no more of 'em. I want my wife!" he cries. Then he encounters Hazel's mother, who lives in Dover. He turns his back on her accusations and heads back to Doc's house with the net.

There Doc reveals that he never believed Hazel had jumped in the river. Angry and frustrated, William heads for home, while Virgil trails along and tries to calm him. "I'm the only man alive knows Hazel," he declares, "I say she would [jump in the river]." The two scuffle, then continue home. William sees an unusual sight over his house: a rainbow at night. Inside, he hears someone call his name. It is Hazel; she has been hiding in the house all day. She watched William reading the note from her hiding place. After dinner, the two sit on their porch. William playfully turns Hazel over on his knee and spanks her, then cradles her in his arms. "It was the same as any other chase in the end," Welty says. The couple heads into their house. ❀

List of Characters in
"The Wide Net"

William Wallace Jamieson, the protagonist, arrives home after a night out to find his wife, Hazel, missing and a suicide note from her declaring that she is going to drown herself. With his friend Virgil, he organizes a search party to drag the river. At the end of the day, he discovers that Hazel has been hiding in their house all along.

Hazel Jamieson, William Wallace's pregnant wife, writes but does not finish a suicide note after her husband has stayed out all night. She hides in the house all day, unaware that her husband is dragging the river for her.

Virgil Thomas is William Wallace's friend and his companion on the night he stays out until morning. He helps William assemble a search party among the townspeople. Later, William tussles with him to make him admit that the search party had been William's idea alone.

Old Doc is the philosophical owner of the wide net, which William borrows to drag the Pearl River. Although he doesn't believe that Hazel has drowned herself, he accompanies the search party, and only admits his belief after the search ends.

The Malones and *the Doyles* are large families whose members are recruited to help drag the river.

Grady and *Brucie Rippen* are young brothers whose father drowned in the Pearl River; Virgil persuades William Wallace to let them join the search party.

Sam and *Robbie Bell* are two black boys who also join the search party. ❀

Critical Views on
"The Wide Net"

DIANA TRILLING ON *THE WIDE NET AND OTHER STORIES*

[Diana Trilling (1905–1996) was a freelance writer and critic. She authored the column "Fiction in Review" in the *Nation* from 1941–1949. Here, Trilling discusses "The Wide Net" in relation to the other stories from the collected work, *The Wide Net and Other Stories.*]

The title story of Miss Welty's new volume is its best story, but not typical. An account of a river-dragging party which starts out to recover the body of a supposed suicide but forgets its mission in the joys of the occasion, "The Wide Net" has its share of the elements of a tour de force, but it has more communicated meaning than the rest of the stories in the book, and it best fuses content and method. Of the six stories "Livvie" is the only one which I like at all, and the only story, in addition to "The Wide Net," which I feel I understood. Yet the volume as a whole has tremendous emotional impact, despite its obscurity. However, this seems to me to be beside the point, for the fear that a story or a picture engenders is likely to be in inverse proportion to its rational content: witness the drawings of children or psychotics, or most of surrealist art; and Miss Welty employs to good effect the whole manual of ghostliness—wind and storm, ruined buildings, cloaks, horses' hooves on a lonely highway, fire and moonlight and people who live and ride alone. But the evocation of the mood of horror or of a dreamlike atmosphere has become an end in itself, and if, for each story, there is a point of departure in narrative, so that I can report, for instance, that "First Love" is about a deaf-and-dumb boy who falls in love with Aaron Burr, or that "Asphodel" is about a tyrannical half-mad Southern gentlewoman, or that "A Still Moment" is a legend of Audubon, still the stories themselves stay with their narrative no more than a dance, say, stays with its argument. This, indeed, is the nature of *The Wide Net*: it is a book of ballets, not of stories; even the title piece is a *pastorale macabre.*

> —Diana Trilling, "'The Wide Net and Other Stories," *Nation*,
> (October 1943): pp. 386–87. ☙

Robert Penn Warren on Love and Separateness in Eudora Welty's Fiction

[Robert Penn Warren (1905–1989) was professor at Yale University in New Haven, Connecticut. He was a recipient of two Pulitzer Prizes: the 1947 fiction prize for *All the King's Men* and the 1958 poetry prize for *Promises: Poems 1954–1956*. In this excerpt, Warren discusses the multiple dimensions of "The Wide Net."]

[W]hen William Wallace, in "The Wide Net," goes out to dredge the river, he is presumably driven by the fear that his wife has jumped in, but the fear is absorbed into the world of the river, and in a saturnalian revel he prances about with a great catfish hung on his belt, like a river-god laughing and leaping. But he had also dived deep down into the water: "Had he suspected down there, like some secret, the real true trouble that Hazel had fallen into, about which words in a letter could not speak . . . how (who knew?) she had been filled to the brim with that elation that they all remembered, like their own secret, the elation that comes of great hopes and changes, sometimes simply of the harvest time, that comes with a little course of its own like a tune to run in the head, and there was nothing she could do about it, they knew—and so it had turned into this? It could be nothing but the old trouble that William Wallace was finding out, reaching and turning in the gloom of such depths."

This passage comes clear when we recall that Hazel, the wife who is supposed to have committed suicide by drowning, is pregnant; she had sunk herself in the devouring life-flux, has lost her individuality there, just as the men hunting for the body have lost the meaning of their mission. For the river is simply force, which does not have its own definition; in it are the lost string of beads to wind around the little Negro boy's head, the catfish for the feast, the baby alligator that looks "like the oldest and worst lizard," and the great King of the Snakes. As Doc, the wise old man who owns the net, says: "The outside world is full of endurance." And he also says: "The excursion is the same when you go looking for your sorrow as when you go looking for your joy." Man has the definition, the dream, but when he plunges into the river he runs the risk of having it washed away. But it is important to notice that in this story, there is not horror at the basic contrast, but a kind of gay acceptance of the issue: when

William Wallace gets home he finds that his wife had fooled him, and spanks her, and then she lies smiling in the crook of his arm. "It was the same as any other chase in the end."

—Robert Penn Warren, *Eudora Welty* (New York: Chelsea House Publishers, 1986): pp. 24–25.

D. JAMES NEAULT ON TIME IN THE FICTION OF EUDORA WELTY

[D. James Neault is the author of several essays on Ezra Pound, including "Richard of St. Victor and Rock Drill." He has also written a number of scholarly studies on Latin subjects. In this excerpt, Neault discusses the spontaneousness of time in Welty's fiction.]

The dislocation of time is deliberate. In "Short Stories," Miss Welty expresses her admiration for D. H. Lawrence, who disrupts chronology to "enter the magical world of pure sense, of evocation"; and for Faulkner, who refuses "to confine the story to its proper time sequence . . . *whole* time bulges at the cracks to get in to the present-time of the story." She believes that art is of value only as it is able to convey the all-encompassing timelessness of the "temporal now":

> . . . the novel from the start has been bound up in the local, the "real," the present, the ordinary day-to-day of human experience. Where the imagination comes in is in directing the use of all this. That use is endless, and there are only four words, of all the millions that we've hatched, that a novel rules out: "Once upon a time." They make a story a fairy tale by the simple sweep of the remove—by abolishing the present and the place where we are instead of conveying them to us. Of course we shall have some sort of fairy tale with us always—just now it is the historical novel. Fiction is properly at work on the here and now, or the past made here and now; for in novels *we* have to be there.

The techniques that Miss Welty employs to create in fiction a "still moment" that is perceived in the eternal present are in the tradition of Flaubert, Bergson, Proust, Joyce, and Faulkner; the use to which Miss Welty directs those techniques is individual [. . .]

Miss Welty's use of myth and mythic allusion ranges from the explicit use of the Circe episode of *The Odyssey* to the more tenuous allusion to Dionysian fertility rites in "The Wide Net." Even a story such as "The Bride of the Innisfallen," apparently free from mythic allusion (aside from that imparted to it by its title), is suggestive of an odyssey, a physical as well as metaphysical search. By the use of myth, Miss Welty succeeds in coalescing all time into the present of the story so as to symbolically unite disparate chronological periods; and by rendering symbolically character in myth-related backgrounds, she is able to make them timeless. . . . Equally important, however, is that Miss Welty's stories do not succeed or fail on the credibility or acceptance of the allusion.

—D. James Neault, *A Still Moment: Essays on the Art of Eudora Welty* (Metuchen, N.J.: Scarecrow Press, Inc., 1978): pp. 44–45.

HARRIET POLLACK ON WELTY, HER STYLE, AND HER AUDIENCE

[Harriet Pollack is a professor at Sweet Briar College in Virginia. She has published essays in various literary journals, including the *Mississippi Quarterly.* Here, Pollack suggests that Welty's departure from common literary conventions in "The Wide Net" may deceive her readers.]

In Jonathan Culler's terms, the text bids the reader to draw on his "literary competence." This competence, which is a knowledge of implicit but well-recognized literary conventions, allows a reader to recognize a story pattern, plot type, or genre, to identify a technique of point of view or an allusion and, on the basis of expectations cued by the test, to predict a kind of meaning to be made. In a successful reading, these conventions are the shared knowledge of the author and reader. Otherwise we have the case of the inexperienced student reader of "The Wide Net" who is perplexed when William Wallace, searching for the remains of his wife Hazel, wanders into the pleasures of a golden day. This none too hypothetical reader, perhaps unfamiliar with the conventions of the heroic epic, cannot predict that the wandering of a hero may prove to be his track, the path by which he will arrive where he is going. In Culler's view, conventional literary expectations make reading and writing possible. These

> The author can write against, certainly . . . may attempt to subvert, but [they are] none the less the context within which his activity takes place, as surely as the failure to keep a promise is made possible by the institution of promising. Choices between words, between sentences, between different modes of presentation, will be made on the basis of their effects; and the notion of effect presupposes modes of reading which are not random or haphazard. Even if an author does not think of readers, he is himself a reader of his own work and will not be satisfied with it unless he can read it as producing effects.

Here, Culler is able to grant the reader his place in the literary process while affirming that the author's text guides his expectations.

> —Harriet Pollack, *Welty: A Life in Literature* (Jackson, Miss.: University Press of Mississippi, 1987): pp. 56–57.

ALBERT J. DEVLIN ON MEETING THE WORLD IN *DELTA WEDDING*

[Albert J. Devlin is a professor of English at the University of Missouri, Columbia. His publications include *Eudora Welty's Chronicle: A Story of Mississippi Life, Conversations with Tennessee Williams,* and essays on Faulkner. He served as guest editor for the special Welty edition of the *Mississippi Quarterly.* In this excerpt, Devlin compares the marital relationship in "The Wide Net" with that of Welty's 1946 novel, *Delta Wedding.*]

Each of the love stories turns on the same marital pivot: the rash deed of a husband—William Wallace carousing all night; George on the trestle with "the look of having been on a debauch"—provokes a sensitive wife to "get back at her husband" by running away. Hazel and Robbie leave notes, and while the former threatens to drown herself in the Pearl River, both expect to raise alarms and to be searched for. Most importantly, each story is set in a "changing-time," as Doc says in "The Wide Net," when human and natural cycles undergo mysterious transformation. Hazel Jamieson is going to have a baby in six months; Robbie wonders if she too has "a child insider her" as she watches George face down the Yellow Dog train.

These materials, perfectly cast in "The Wide Net," are remodeled in Delta Wedding to fit the more spacious design of the novel. Robbie Reid, the runaway, unexpectedly replaces William Wallace as searcher; and several of his perceptions of Hazel are redirected, nearly verbatim, to George Fairchild. These substitutions have the important effect of allowing Welty to refocus William Wallace's halting grasp of his wife's trouble.

> Had he suspected down there [in "the dark water"] . . . the real, the true trouble that Hazel had fallen into, about which words in a letter could not speak . . . how (who knew?) she had been filled to the brim with that elation that . . . comes of great hopes and changes . . . It could be nothing but the old trouble that William Wallace was finding out, reaching and turning in the gloom of such depth.

> —Albert J. Devlin, *Critical Essays on Eudora Welty* (Boston: G. K. Hall & Co., 1989): pp. 99–100.

BARBARA HARRELL CARSON ON STORIES OF INITIATION

[Barbara Harrell Carson is a professor of English at Rollins College in Winter Park, Florida. She has held a fellowship from the National Endowment for the Humanities (NEH) and has been named an Arthur Vining Davis Fellow. She has also published articles on Bronson Alcott and Anne Tyler. In this excerpt, Carson examines Welty's development of "individual separateness" in her characters.]

Since "The Wide Net," the final story of this initiation group, is a comedy, it is fitting that it treat with comic reversal the vision at the center of the other stories. Here William Wallace goes to his initiation confident of his ability to untie with the mystery of the other. He is absolutely sure he understands his wife Hazel. What he learns instead is the other, but equally true, side of reality: that beneath apparent human unity there is always the mystery of individual separateness.

The other main components of the ritual remain the same. William Wallace is readied for a new view of life by the shock of his wife's supposed suicide. Preparing to drag the Pearl River for her body, he and his friend enter "in silence" the deep, dim, still woods, stepping "among the great walls of vines and among the passionflowers." By the river stands the now familiar tree, this time a magnolia, under which William Wallace and his companions take shelter. The magnolia responds to the pounding of the rain by releasing its fragrance without yielding its strength.

As in the other stories, symbolic revelations of unity cascade before the initiate. Doc (the hierophant here) suggests that they are at the interface between time and eternity, at the meeting point of life and death, ripeness and decay, when he describes the world as all of one color, frozen gold for just one moment before the changes of autumn occur. (The image works in much the same way as Nina's description of the perfect pear in "Moon Lake.") At the Pearl River, silence turns out really to be its opposite: "The thing that seemed like silence must have been the endless cry of all the crickets and locusts in the world, rising and falling." Doc (who is never really concerned that Hazel has killed herself, but who knows that William Wallace has to discover reality for himself) voices the ultimate paradox when he says: "The excursion is the same when you go looking for your sorrow as when you go looking for your joy." And in a transformation symbolic of the union of the human and natural worlds, each member of the search party is plastered with wet leaves, causing the young boy Sammy to wail, "Now us got scales . . . Us is the fishes." Later, William Wallace manifests a similar unifying vision when, walking home, he sees all the women he has known as "all one young girl standing up to sing under the trees the oldest and longest ballads there were."

—Barbara Harrell Carson, *Eudora Welty: Two Pictures at Once in Her Frame* (New York: The Whitston Publishing Company, 1992): pp. 45–46.

Plot Summary of
"No Place for You, My Love"

This short story opens at a restaurant luncheon on a sweltering Sunday afternoon in New Orleans. A man and a woman, two Northerners whom the author never names, are seated side by side at the luncheon. They are strangers to one another and to the city. Most of the story takes place in the minds of these self-conscious characters, who spend a day together in an environment completely foreign to them before they return to New Orleans and part company.

As the story begins, the man is reflecting silently on the woman's appearance and behavior. He guesses that she has had an affair with a married man. He doesn't like the hat she is wearing. The woman thinks that her being in love "must stick out all over me . . . so people think they can love me or hate me just by looking at me." He makes idle conversation with her by remarking that they both seem to have weak appetites, and she claims that the heat is responsible.

The man offers to take her on a drive heading south of the city. They leave the restaurant and he escorts her to his rented Ford. They thread through New Orleans "as though following the clue in a maze" and head for a concrete highway bordered by a levee, a tangle of undergrowth, and a few settlements. Welty describes at length the transition in scenery from city to suburbs to outskirts as the man speeds south. At one point, the woman nudges him as he begins to doze off in the oppressive heat.

They arrive at a levee and at the last minute are able to board a ferry with the rented car. The rest of the passengers are boisterous and seem to know one another. As the ferry pulls away with a piercing whistle, the woman's hat blows off. The man, who was still in the car on the deck below her, retrieves it and brings it to her. The rest of the passengers, meanwhile, stare at the couple and try to figure out where they have come from.

When they reach the opposite shore in late afternoon, they feel as though "they had been racing around an arena in their chariot, among lions." As they continue driving, the man wonders whether his companion is wishing that someone else were with them, her husband or lover, perhaps. The heat intensifies, and shimmers as if alive. They discuss it briefly, and the woman feels a sudden panic. "How dear—how costly—could this ride be?" she wonders.

Eventually, the paved road turns into a track paved with white shells. They pass through a cemetery filled with fresh flowers and see a small church, a house with a newly caught catfish on its doorstep, and a priest's gown hanging on a clothesline. "What is your wife like?" the woman suddenly asks the man. He raises his hand but does not reply. The priest steps outside, looks at the couple, then goes back into the house. The man backs out of the cemetery and continues to head south as the sun sets.

Along the way an old man flags them down and tells them that they have reached the road's end. Before long they come upon a row of shacks. They get out of the car and head toward the water. The central shack has a beer sign hanging in the window that says "Baba's Place." The moon is rising, and a few local men are standing near the water.

The man and woman enter Baba's Place. The other patrons are engaged in a card game. At the bar, the two strangers examine their surroundings as they wait for service. A man whom they presume to be Baba serves the man a beer and a sandwich. The woman asks for water, but Baba brings her another sandwich and beer. She notices that she is attracting attention from other patrons. Soon a crowd of adults and children make their way into the shack. They are cleanly dressed and appear to have come from church services. The man is summoned to the table of card players, where one man apologizes for having made a remark while "there was a lady present."

Welty describes the atmosphere of the tiny restaurant in great detail: the local regulars, the smells of the kitchen, Baba's laughter, the sounds of nickels in the slot machines and of the jukebox, the dog lying in front of the jukebox with "his ribs working fast as a concertina's" from the heat. Soon, no one seems to notice the two strangers at the bar.

After a while, the woman slides off her stool to go outside for fresh air, but the man grabs her wrist and begins to dance with her. The woman realizes that the man can probably see the large bruise at her temple and decides that it is his due for having silenced her question about his wife. Welty describes the couple's dancing as the unconscious focal point of their journey: "They had found it, and had almost missed it: they had had to dance. They were what their separate hearts desired that day, for themselves and each other."

A goose wanders aimlessly onto the dance floor and is lured away by children. At length, the man and woman stand on the porch to take in the night air before going on their way. They ride without speaking back to New Orleans. The man stops once to clean the windshield of bugs. He stops a second time and kisses the woman. When he begins driving again, he feels as though they are riding "across a face—great, wide, and upturned." The woman appears to be asleep. He increases his speed.

Back in the bustling city of New Orleans, the man becomes momentarily disoriented, but finds his way to the hotel where the woman is staying. He has been thinking that neither one of them will ever tell the story of their excursion this day, because to do so would be to make it less "incredible." At the hotel entrance, he begins to apologize by saying "Forgive . . ." but does not finish. "And that was just what she did," says the author, "forgive him." The man sits a while in his rented car, remembers that he is staying in New Orleans for the night, and realizes that the city's night life is just beginning. He heads back to his own hotel. The bustle reminds him of his student days in New York, when the "shriek and horror and unholy smother of the subway had its original meaning for him as the lilt and expectation of love." ❁

List of Characters in
"No Place for You, My Love"

The Man is a visitor from Syracuse, New York, who is attending a luncheon in New Orleans. He is seated next to a woman he does not know, and he asks her to accompany him on a ride heading south.

The Woman is from Toledo, Ohio. She agrees to accompany the man on a ride in his rented car. The reader learns that the hat she is wearing disguises a bruise on her temple.

Baba is the owner of a small restaurant at the end of the road that the man and woman have been driving on. ✿

Critical Views on
"No Place for You, My Love"

RUTH M. VANDE KIEFT ON WELTY'S MATURITY OF STYLE

[Ruth M. Vande Kieft is a professor of English at Queens College of the City University of New York. She is a personal friend of Eudora Welty's and has been publishing material on Welty's life and career for more than 30 years. Kieft also edited Welty's *Thirteen Stories.* Here she examines the author's writing style.]

It is difficult to isolate the changes in Miss Welty's style without considering their relation to character, situation, and point of view. The sophistication of style in "No Place for You, My Love," for example, is fitted to the sophistication of the two main characters and their situation: two self-conscious modern people, briefly whirled together and then apart, whose relationship is determined by the nature of the environment they encounter together and by the heat and speed of their journey, as much as by their own natures. The self-consciousness of the relationship invades, or pervades, the style. Even the metaphors are affected, and some of them are difficult to interpret, as, for instance, the following, which appears toward the end of the story, just after the couple have returned to New Orleans and are about to leave each other: "Something that must have been with them all along suddenly, then, was not. In a moment, tall as panic, it rose, cried like a human, and dropped back." Without the help of Miss Welty's explanation in "How I Write," one might puzzle over that metaphor long and fruitlessly. She says the cry was that of "the fading relationship—personal, individual, psychic—admitted in order to be denied, a cry that the characters were first able (and prone) to listen to, and then able in part to ignore. The cry was authentic to my story and so I didn't care if it did seem a little odd: the end of a journey can set up a cry, the shallowest provocation to sympathy and love does hate to give up the ghost." The metaphor is odd, but it was born legitimately out of an odd story with an odd point of view.

It is, finally, the storyteller who reveals sophistication in the stories of *The Bride of the Innisfallen:* a writer who is far more aware of multiple choices, the varieties of form and technique possible to the creative imagination, than was the writer of *A Curtain of Green*. As an artist, Miss Welty seems to have gone through the kind of change she has so often described in her fiction: the passage from innocence to experience. What is lost in this process is simplicity, purity, lucidity, immediacy in relation to the materials of fiction, a natural and instinctive grace, an intuitive perception and realization of form, and relative ease and spontaneity of creation. The sophistication which is gained at the expense of the loss of innocence has a compensating value: the stories provide the delight which comes from the experience of an art beautifully and skillfully executed, varied, mature, experimental. And throughout, the power of feeling has never been lost.

> —Ruth M. Vande Kieft, *Eudora Welty* (New York: Twayne Publishers, Inc., 1962): pp. 158–59.

ALUN R. JONES ON WELTY'S EXILED CHARACTERS

[Alun R. Jones has published material in various literary journals, including *Shenandoah,* where this excerpt originally appeared. In this extract, Jones discusses the sense of exile in Welty's characters.]

In "No Place for You, My Love," the Eastern business man and the girl from the Middle West are thrown together because they are "strangers to each other, and both fairly well strangers to the place." Miss Welty emphasises their shared sense of exile and their feeling of the hostility of New Orleans. The girl's "naive face" seemed to say "Show me," in contrast to the "Southern look—Southern mask—of life-is-a-dream irony, which could turn to pure challenge at the drop of a hat." Yet the author does not identify with her characters, who have surprisingly little to say to each other, but with the landscape through which they drive. This landscape itself takes on the atmosphere of a dream as if all roads going South from New Orleans led to the edge of the world, to the very borders of consciousness.

Existence in this elemental world is dominated by light so intense that it is felt as weight and heat so stifling and claustrophobic that it seems to imprison all who enter. The roads themselves are paved with seashells and the inhabitants wait for the Shrimp Dance to begin as if they lived in that uncharted, amphibious region when life first emerged from the sea on to the shores of consciousness. They return to the world with a sense of some profound mysterious experience they have shared like mythical voyagers returned from the underworld,

> A thing is incredible, if ever, only after it is told—returned to the world it came out of. For their different reasons, he thought, neither of them would tell this (unless something was dropped out of them): that, strangers, they had ridden down into a strange land together and were setting safely back—by a slight margin, perhaps, but margin enough. . . .
> Something that must have been with them all along suddenly, then, was not. In a moment, tall as panic, it rose, cried like a human, and dropped back.

This "something" embodied that elemental relationship that grows up between these two strangers, who together visited the very borders of consciousness, and who came to know and accepted an order of being utterly remote from their everyday life, falls away like some shade from out of Hades as they return to the known world and a different order of reality. Thus although the man, at least, recovers a memory of innocence as keen as love, he also relinquishes his knowledge of a profound order of being that exists below and beyond the world in which people have names, occupations and families.

> —Alun R. Jones, "A Frail Travelling Coincidence: Three Later Stories of Eudora Welty," in *Critical Essays on Eudora Welty* (Boston: G. K. Hall, 1989): pp. 185–86.

ALBERT J. GRIFFITH ON EUDORA WELTY'S LITERARY THEORY

[Albert J. Griffith is a professor of English and Vice President and Dean of Academic Affairs at Our Lady of the Lake University in San Antonio, Texas. He is the author of a critical study of Peter Taylor, as well as numerous critical essays. In this excerpt, Griffith examines Welty's "mysteriousness" in fiction.]

Miss Welty's concept of mysteriousness in fiction is, perhaps, the clue both to the vagaries of her language and the nebulousness of her themes. This double element of ambiguity is purposive, intended to correspond to the equivocation of esthetic emotions, which speak both to the conscious and the subconscious mind, despite "quondam obstruction." "We are speaking of beauty," she says, "and beauty is not a blatant or promiscuous or obvious quality—indeed at her finest she is somehow associated with obstruction—with reticence of a number of kinds." The first thing a reader sees in a story is this fascinating attribute of mystery. "Every good story has mystery—not the puzzle kind, but the mystery of allurement," she insists. "As we understand the story better, it's likely that the mystery does not necessarily decrease; rather it simply grows more beautiful."

But Miss Welty does not make the pursuit of mystery an indiscriminating excuse for obscurity. It is true that she praises that "sense of opaqueness" found in masters of the short story like Faulkner ("Faulkner's prose, let's suspect, is intolerantly and intolerably unanalysable and quite pure . . . with its motes bright-pure and dark-pure falling on us"), D. H. Lawrence ("the atmosphere that cloaks D. H. Lawrence's stories is pure but thick cover, a cloak of self-luminous air"), and Hemingway ("action can be inscrutable, more than sensation can . . . just as voluptuous, too, just as vaporous and, as I am able to see it, much more desperately concealing"). Yet she can also praise Glenway Wescott because "everywhere is the dignity of a style in which there is nothing wasteful and nothing wanting in saying an explicit thing." And, for affecting stylistic obscurantism inadroitly, she takes to task authors like Edita Morris ("the author seems to be writing too delicately, in order to keep her distance from such extraordinary characters, that we seem especially to notice her tiptoeing") and Dorothy Baker ("her indistinct, often careless, sometimes ungrammatical sentences show a disregard for accuracy and clarity in the interest of manner and mannerism"). In her own stories, Miss Welty has been careful to try to merge or identify the abstract (including that desirable mysteriousness) with the concrete. She has revealed that in the reworking of "No Place for You, My Love," she cut some "odd" sentences out of it, "not because they were odd—for the story is that—but because they would tantalize some cooling explanations out of the mind if they stayed in." "I had no wish to sound mystical," she proclaims, "but I did expect to sound mysterious now and then, if I could: this was a circumstantial, realistic story in which the reality was mystery."

—Albert Griffith, *A Still Moment: Essays on the Art of Eudora Welty* (Metuchen, N.J.: Scarecrow Press, Inc., 1978): pp. 58–59.

BARBARA HARRELL CARSON ON WELTY'S "TANGLED BANK"

[Barbara Harrell Carson is a professor of English at Rollins College in Winter Park, Florida. She has held a fellowship from the National Endowment for the Humanities (NEH) and has been named an Arthur Vining Davis Fellow. She has also published articles on Bronson Alcott and Anne Tyler. In this excerpt, Carson explores Welty's emphasis on a non-dual reality.]

The encounter with non-dual reality in "No Place for You, My Love" also occurs on the banks of the Mississippi. Once again the initiates are cut off from ordinary human communication and are made susceptible to new insights by their less than satisfactory lives. Both Northerners in the South and strangers to each other, the unnamed woman and man have each apparently suffered a recent weakening of their ties with those they love. Her bruised temple suggests a troubled love affair; his wife's suggestion that he stay out from underfoot while she entertains old college friends speaks for a less than harmonious marriage. Together the strangers retreat from Galatoir's to Baba's Place in the Delta, a trip to a locale that seems "out of this world," "a sort of dead man's land, where nobody came." In the process, each enters that familiar dream-like state. Signaling the diminishment of civilized order and restraint, he loosens his collar and tie; she momentarily loses her hat. Clearly this is, as he declares, a "Time Out" from their usual lives.

The levee holding back the Mississippi becomes one wall effecting their enclosure. The feeling of insularity is increased by the "uprooted trees . . . drawn across their path, sawing at the air and tumbling one over the other." The tangled bank they enter is straight from scenes of primordial chaos. As Mircea Eliade points out, all initiations involve a re-enactment of creation and "every ritual repetition of the cosmogony is preceded by a symbolic retrogression to Chaos." This return to the original condition before division into parts has been, of course, part of the *raison d'être* of all of Welty's retreats to the tangled bank. In "No Place for You, My Love," just as before the first order of creation, earth and water blend together. The river itself feels "like the sea" and looks "like the earth." The land is "strange . . . amphibious and whether water-covered or grown with jungle or robbed entirely of water and trees . . . it had the same loneliness." At the end of the road "there was water under everything. Even where a screen of jungle had been left to stand, splashes could be heard from under the trees. In the vast open, sometimes boats moved inch by inch through what appeared endless meadows of rubbery flowers."

—Barbara Harrell Carson, "Eudora Welty's Tangled Bank," *South Atlantic Review* 48, No. 4 (November 1983): pp. 10–11.

RUTH M. VANDE KIEFT ON THE QUEST IN WELTY'S SHORT STORIES

[Ruth M. Vande Kieft is a professor of English at Queens College of the City University of New York. She is a personal friend of Eudora Welty's and has been publishing material on Welty's life and career for more than 30 years. Kieft also edited Welty's *Thirteen Stories*. In this excerpt, Vande Kieft reviews the recurring theme of a journey in Welty's short stories.]

"The Bride of the Innisfallen," "No Place for You, My Love," and "Going to Naples" are . . . stories of quest or journey. But whose is each journey, why is it taken, what is its significance? In ["The Bride of the Innisfallen"] the central character is not, as might be expected, the bride, but the American girl for whom the bride, never identified, seems to represent love at its pristine moment of joy, hope, expectancy. Contrasted with the motivations of Phoenix or William Wallace, her motivation for taking the journey is as obscure as her central "problem." . . . An excess of hope and joy, an openness to life, expectation and outgoing love of it, have become a burden on her heart because these feelings cannot be shared or acted upon. This motivation is not incomprehensible: it seems to me both credible and moving. But it is somewhat rarefied and difficult for the reader to discover, especially outside the context of Eudora Welty's work as a whole; and part of this difficulty is the lack of the immediate, tangible human relationships found in "A Worn Path" or "The Wide Net."

A similar vagueness surrounds the flight of the young woman in "No Place for You, My Love." We know only from the Easterner's point of view, that back home she must be involved in some hopeless love relationship (possibly with a married man), that there may recently have been a "scene," since she has on her temple a bruise which affects her "like an evil star," that her frantic need is for escape and the protection of distance and anonymity, and that her painful obsession is with exposure. But if the heroine's situation is vague, we know from Eudora Welty's account in "Writing and Analyzing a Story" that it is intended to be; we also know that the point of view was neither the woman's nor her companion's but that of a mysterious third presence:

> It was . . . fished alive from the surrounding scene. As I wrote further into the story, something more real, more essential, than the characters were on their own was revealing itself. In effect . . . there had come to be a sort of third character along on the ride—the presence of a relationship between the two. It was what grew up between them meeting as strangers, went on the excursion with them. . . . I wanted to suggest that its being took shape as the strange, compulsive journey itself, was palpable as its climate and mood, the heat of the day. . . .
>
> I wanted to make seen and believed what was to me, in my story's grip, literally apparent—that secret and shadow are taken away in this country by the merciless light that prevails there, by the river that is like an exposed vein of ore, the road that descends as one with the heat—its nerve (these are all terms in the story), and that the heat is also a visual illusion, shimmering and dancing over the waste that stretches ahead. . . . I was writing of exposure, and the shock of the world; in the end I tried to make the story's inside outside and then leave the shell behind.

Eudora Welty accomplished what she set out to do, but it was a perilous undertaking. She took a human feeling—a panicky, raw-nerved sense of exposure—and invested an entire landscape and journey with that feeling; she rendered a strong emotional effect without supplying much information about its cause. The vivid impressionism of this method is strangely exciting, but the story is not as fully and solidly alive as is a story like "A Worn Path," in which there seems never to have been a shell to leave behind because every part—plot, character, setting, theme—seems essential to every other part.

—Ruth M. Vande Kieft, *Eudora Welty* (Boston: Twayne Publishers, 1987): pp. 127–28.

RUTH D. WESTON ON THE GOTHIC SPACE AS NARRATIVE TECHNIQUE

[Ruth D. Weston is a professor of English at Oral Roberts University. She has published various essays and a book on Eudora Welty. In this excerpt, Weston discusses landscape in Welty's fiction.]

Whatever function Welty gives the landscape, the space itself has as much significance as the human characters. Welty has said, in her own analysis of "No Place for You, My Love," that its atmosphere, which is based on the reality of the unclear border between the natural elements of land, water, and air in the Louisiana delta, is so nearly tangible as to constitute a "third character" in the plot. The charged atmosphere, which holds the two northern travelers as if they were in an active chemical medium, is a character, Welty says, in the sense that it plays the role of a relationship between the man from Syracuse and the woman from Toledo. The idea that the third character will play a powerful role is introduced early in the story during a mediation on the propriety of the two strangers' taking a side trip from their chance meeting in New Orleans: "Had she felt a wish for someone else to be riding with them? . . . Whatever people like to think, situations (if not scenes) were usually three-way—there was somebody else always. The one who didn't—couldn't—understand the two made *the formidable third*" (Welty's emphasis). They are slowly seduced by this "third" as they cross the ferry, drive through "a sort of dead man's land, where nobody came," and approach each other tentatively. Their point of closest communication is at the appropriately named beer shack Baba's Place in Venice, Louisiana; for this is a never-never land as far from their ordinary lives as that of Ali Baba's adventures. Even the ferry boat has seemed in a "trance," and on board are two boys with a chained alligator, described as "the last worldly evidence of some old heroic horror of the dragon." The spell of Baba's Place temporarily makes the woman into a heroine, as "she accepted it that she was more beautiful or perhaps more fragile than the women they saw every day of their lives." And the terror of gothic cruelty is not missing from the story either, though Welty's glancing narrative skims by it: as the couple dance, "she became aware that he could not help but see the bruise at her temple. . . . She felt it come out like an evil star." It is a sign, perhaps, of a cruel relationship from which she has fled. Although they dance like "professional, Spanish dancers wearing masks," the mysterious neutral ground of the beer shack, condensed in the bare stage of the dance floor and further condensed in the circle of their own arms, allows the masks to drop for a significant moment: "Surely even those immune from the world, for the time being, need the touch of one another, or all is lost. Their arms encircling each other, their bodies circling the odorous, just-nailed-down floor, they were, at last, imperviousness in motion. They had found it, and had almost missed it: they had had to dance. They were what their separate hearts desired that day, for themselves and each other."

—Ruth D. Weston, *Gothic Traditions and Narrative Techniques in the Fiction of Eudora Welty* (Baton Rouge and London: Louisiana State University Press, 1994): pp. 37–38.

Works by
Eudora Welty

A Curtain of Green and Other Stories. 1941.
The Robber Bridegroom. 1942.
The Wide Net and Other Stories. 1943.
Delta Wedding. 1946.
Music from Spain. 1948.
Short Stories. 1949.
The Golden Apples. 1949.
The Ponder Heart. 1954.
The Bride of the Innisfallen and Other Stories. 1955.
Place in Fiction. 1957.
Three Papers on Fiction. 1962.
The Shoe Bird. 1964.
Thirteen Stories. Ed. Ruth Vende Kieft. 1965.
A Sweet Devouring. 1969.
A Flock of Guinea Hens Seen from a Car. 1970.
Losing Battles. 1970.
One Time, One Place: Mississippi in the Depression: A Snapshot Album. 1971.
The Optimist's Daughter. 1973.
A Pageant of Birds. 1975.
Fairy Tale of the Natchez Trace. 1975.
The Eye of the Story: Selected Essays and Reviews. 1975.
Ida M'Toy. 1979.
Moon Lake and Other Stories. 1980.
The Collected Stories of Eudora Welty. 1980.
Miracles of Perception: The Art of Willa Cather (with Alfred Knopf and Yehudi Menuhin). 1980.
Retreat. 1981.
Conversations with Eudora Welty. Ed. Peggy Whitman Prenshaw. 1984.
One Writer's Beginnings. 1984.
The Little Store. 1985.
More Conversations with Eudora Welty. Ed. Peggy Whitman Prenshaw. 1996.

Works about
Eudora Welty

Brinkmeyer, Robert H., Jr. "An Openness to Otherness: The Imaginative Vision of Eudora Welty." *Southern Literary Journal*, XX (1988): 69–80.

Brooks, Cleanth, and Robert Penn Warren. *Understanding Fiction*. New Haven: Prentice-Hall, 1966.

Carson, Barbara Harrell. *Eudora Welty: Two Pictures at Once in Her Frame*. Troy, NY: The Whitston Publishing Company, 1992.

Cash, W. J. *The Mind of the South*. New York: Peter Smith Publishers, 1941.

Chase, Richard V. *The American Novel and Its Tradition*. Garden City, NJ: Gordian Press, 1957.

Desmond, John F. *A Still Moment: Essays on the Art of Eudora Welty*. Metuchen, NJ: Scarecrow Press, 1978.

Devlin, Albert J. *Eudora Welty's Chronicle: A Story of Mississippi Life*. Jackson, MS: University Press of Mississippi, 1983.

Evans, Elizabeth. *Eudora Welty*. New York: Ungar Publishing, 1981.

Ferguson, Mary Anne. "The Female Novel of Development and the Myth of Psyche." *Denver Quarterly*, XVII (1983): 58–74.

Ferris, Bill. *Images of the South: Visits with Eudora Welty and Walker Evans*. Memphis: Southern Folklore Reports Series, No. 1, 1977.

Fleenor, Juliann E. *The Female Gothic*. Montreal: Eden Press, 1983.

Frye, Northrop. *The Anatomy of Criticism*. New York: Princeton University Press, 1970.

Gilligan, Carol. *In a Different Voice: Psychological Theory and Women's Development*. Cambridge, MA: Harvard University Press, 1982.

Haggerty, George E. *Gothic Fiction/Gothic Form*. University Park, PA: Pennsylvania University Press, 1989.

Hardy, John Edward. "*Delta Wedding* as Region and Symbol." *Sewanee Review*, LX (1952): 397–417.

Hoffman, Frederick J. *The Art of Southern Fiction: A Study of Some Modern Novelists*. Carbondale, IL: Southern Illinois University Press, 1967.

Jones, Anne Goodwyn. *Tomorrow is Another Day: The Woman Writer in the South, 1859–1936*. Baton Rouge, LA: Louisiana State University Press, 1981.

Kayser, Wolfgang. *The Grotesque in Art and Literature*. Trans. by Ulrich Weisstein. Bloomington, IL: McGraw-Hill, 1963.

Kestner, Joseph A. *The Spatiality of the Novel*. Detroit: Wayne State University Press, 1978.

Kinnett, David. "Miss Kellogg's Quiet Passion." *Wisconsin Magazine of History*, LXII (1979): 267–99.

Landess, Thomas. "The Function of Taste in the Fiction of Eudora Welty." *Mississippi Quarterly*, XXVI (1973): 543–57.

McDonald, W. U., Jr. Postscript to *Eudora Welty Newsletter*, XII (1988): 15.

Malin, Irving. *The New American Gothic*, Carbondale, IL: Southern Illinois University Press, 1962.

Mississippi Quarterly 26 (Fall 1971). Special Eudora Welty issue.

Moers, Ellen. *Literary Women*. New York: Oxford University Press, 1976.

Oates, Joyce Carol. "The Art of Eudora Welty." *Shenandoah*, XX (1969): 54–57.

Opitz, Kurt. "The Order of a Chaotive Soul." *Critique*, VII (1964–65): 79–91.

Pei, Lowry. "Dreaming the Other in *The Golden Apples*." *Modern Fiction Studies* 28, no. 3 (Autumn 1982): 415–33.

Porter, Katherine Anne. Introduction to *Selected Stories of Eudora Welty*. New York: Modern Library, 1954.

Randisi, Jennifer Lynn. *A Tissue of Lies: Eudora Welty and the Southern Romance*. Washington, DC: University Press of America, 1982.

Rubin, Louis D., Jr. *The History of Southern Literature*. Baton Rouge, LA: Louisiana State University Press, 1985.

Schmidt, Peter. *The Heart of the Story: Eudora Welty's Short Fiction*. Jackson, MS: University Press of Mississippi, 1989.

Snelling, Paula. Review of Eudora Welty's *A Curtain of Green*. *The South Today*, VII (1942): 61.

Tate, Allen. "Techniques of Fiction." In *Essays of Four Decades*. Chicago: Swallow Press, 1968.

Vande Kieft, Ruth M. *Eudora Welty*. Boston: Twayne Publishers, 1962.

Warren, Robert Penn. "Love and Separateness in Eudora Welty." *Kenyon Review,* VI (1944): 245–59.

Young, Thomas Daniel. *The Past in the Present: A Thematic Study of Modern Southern Fiction*. Baton Rouge, LA: Louisiana State University Press, 1981.

Index of
Themes and Ideas